the COLLE

Box

ELIZABETH BRAIMBRIDGE
BOBBY MEYER

Published in 1998

SAGE PRESS,

PO Box Nº 1, Rye, East Sussex TN36 4ZX.
Freephone: 0800 092 33 31
e-mail: summertime @ lineone.net
© Sage Press 1998

All rights reserved.

Set in Palatine italic 9 ½ on 11 point leading.
Display in Monotype Centaur 48 point.

Design and illustrations
Chris Monk of Yellowduck Design & Illustration.

Research
Cindy Stevens

Editor
Cindy Stevens

Series Editor and Publisher
Mrs Bobby Meyer

Printed by Judges Ltd. in Hastings

This book is sold subject to the condition
that it shall not, by way of trade or otherwise,
be lent, re-sold, hired out, or otherwise circulated
without the publisher's prior consent in any form
of binding or cover other than in which it is
published and without a similar condition
including this condition being
imposed on the subsequent purchaser.

ISBN: 0 - 9531644 - 5 - 4

 BOX

"...IF WE EVER LIVED ON ANOTHER ball of stone than this, it must be that there was Box growing on it." *(Oliver Wendell Holmes, Elsie Venner)*

Box, or boxwood, is a tree which excites passions. The formal gardener sings its praises, others find it drab; in gardens, it has been alternately in and out of fashion for centuries; its smell is both loved and loathed.

The Ancient Egyptians imported boxwood from Syria, together with cedar, cypress and ash. Classical Roman gardens made great use of the tree.

In England, archeologists have found evidence of boxwood from Neolithic times. It was mentioned in the Domesday Book, and referred to as a boundary shrub in medieval charters in Hampshire.

The antiquarian (and gossip) John Aubrey, writing of Boxwell, Gloucestershire, in 1685, described "a great wood.....which .....Mr Huntley fells, and sells to the combe-makers in London."

The philosopher John Stuart Mill, among others, noted large stands in the Tring-Dunstable area, planted by the Duke of Bridgwater in the mid-eighteenth century to meet the demand for the wood from London craftsmen.

Two native sites remain, in Surrey and Buckinghamshire, and the common box has left its mark in place-names.

🌿 Place-names

Around twenty English settlements, all in the southern chalklands to which the tree is native, have the prefix 'Box' to their names. There are two Boxfords, a Boxbush and a Boxgrove, among others. Boxley, a famous site near Maidstone in Kent, derives the second part of its name from the Anglo-Saxon for 'clearing'.

There are villages called, simply, Box in Wiltshire and Gloucestershire.

Some other names are also associated with the tree: Bixley, in Norfolk, means 'boxwoods', and Bexington, in Dorset, means 'settlement among box".

Box Hill, in Surrey, has been made famous by Jane Austen in her novel, **Emma**: *"Emma had never been to Box Hill; she wished to see what everybody found so well worth seeing…"*

Earlier, in 1706, the diarist, John Evelyn, had written: "The Ladies, Gentlemen and other Water-Drinkers from the neighbouring Ebesham-Spaw (Spa), often…divert themselves in those Antilex natural Alleys, and shady Recesses, among the Box-trees…"

In 1808, William Gilpin described its "shivering precipices, and downy hillocks, everywhere interspersed with the mellow verdure of box."

The native British box is but one of many varieties in the world - Cuba

alone has thirty species. The trees, or shrubs, are much used in garden design, and its wood is of great value.

🌿 Non-horticultural uses of boxwood

Wood turning and carving

The Latin name for box, **buxus**, *is derived from the Greek* **pyknos** *or* **pyxos**, *meaning a finely carved wooden box. It is a very hard, fine-grained wood, ideal for intricate carving. Many delicately carved religious statuettes were made from boxwood by medieval craftsmen.*

The rootwood, known as dudgeon, is even harder. It is paler in colour than the yellow boxwood, being almost bone-coloured. A major use for it was in the making of dagger handles.

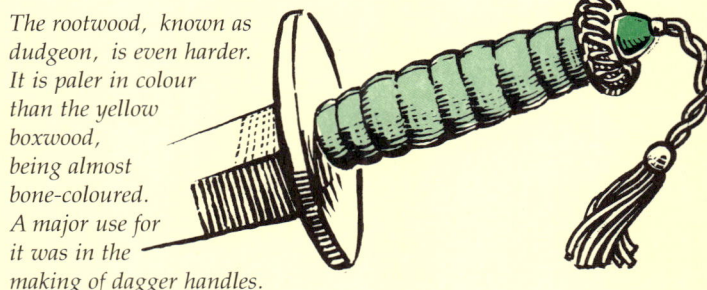

Ancient classical literature mentions boxwood combs and writing tablets, and the use of the wood for inlaying. There are references in the Old Testament. In Isaiah, *boxwood is named with two other trees as decorating the Lord's sanctuary, while* Ezekiel 27.6 *describes a ship: "of the oaks of Bashan they have made thine oars; they have made thy benches of ivory inlaid in boxwood, from the isles of Chittim."*

In The Iliad, Book 24, *Homer refers to boxwood being used for a less decorative purpose, to make a yoke for King Priam's mules.*

Thomas Bewick, the celebrated engraver of natural history subjects in the late eighteenth and early nineteenth centuries, used boxwood blocks for his work. They were cut on the cross of the grain to maximise their hardness and durability, and were ideal for the new fast printing presses because they were so resilient. Bewick claimed to have used one block for 90,000 printings; it was still sound after that. His work was very fine and detailed.

In the 1830s, there was great demand for boxwood to make engraving blocks for illustrations in the popular papers, since the new steam presses were unable to take the old copper engravings alongside type. The woods around London became very valuable with the demand from papers such as the Penny Magazine *and the* Illustrated London News.

In the eighteenth and nineteenth centuries, box was also used to make moulds for picture frames and furniture decoration. Gilded paste was often used for these purposes because handcarving was so costly.

Box is used in marquetry, its yellow colour contrasting well with dark woods like ebony and walnut.

Box was much in demand by the makers of mathematical instruments and rulers. Judging from early schoolboy stories, a rap on the knuckles from a boxwood ruler was indeed a painful experience; perhaps fortunately, later school rulers were made from inferior wood.

Box, being so hard, was used widely for many purposes before steel became available. Shuttles for weaving silk and other fabrics, screws, small wheels and cogs, were some of its industrial uses. Buttons were made from boxwood and it was also used for wooden domestic utensils, or treen. This included elaborately carved items such as sugar-ladles, as well as nutcrackers and more mundane articles such as rolling pins and pestles.

Box was much used in the making of early woodwind instruments such as shawms and early oboes, recorders and early flutes. Later woodwind, such as clarinets, required greater use of metal, having many more keys.

The durability of box made it a popular choice for the construction of children's toys, especially those which were likely to receive much hard use. It was also used for more delicate items such as intricately carved chessmen.

❧ Other uses

Perhaps because of its sombre colouring, box has long been associated with funerals. William Wordsworth described the Lake District custom of throwing box on to the coffin after it was lowered into the grave: a basin of cuttings would be placed by the door of the deceased's house from which mourners would help themselves before the ceremony.

Similar customs continued in North-West England until the late nineteenth century. A Daily Telegraph *reporter covering a colliery disaster near Wigan in November 1868 described the practice, saying that rosemary or thyme would be more usual "but these poor Hindley people not being able to obtain these poetical plants, have, rather than give up an old custom, contented themselves with stripping several trees of boxwood."*

Rather more unusual than these is 'hysteric ale.' This was made with boxwood chips left after wood-turning, iron filings and herbs, and was 'to be taken constantly by vaporous women'. Folklore does not record its effectiveness.

A common modern use of box is the harvesting of young shoots for florists' wreaths.

Box in the wild

The native English box grows best on pure chalk, although it has been found on oolitic limestone. It likes shade and sometimes forms an 'understorey' to taller trees such as beech. It grows well on steep slopes where other trees find it hard to survive.

Box Hill is one of the two remaining native stands ; the other is on the Chequers estate in Buckinghamshire. This was common land until the beginning of the nineteenth century and so the trees were roughly coppiced for firewood. Following enclosure, a tenant wrote: "the box increases in beauty and value and forms a very picturesque appearance." It now consists of ancient trees, and some young saplings, in three steep-sided coombes. In his book, Flora Britannica, *Richard Mabey describes the "extraordinary atmosphere amongst the twisted trunks…filled with that pungent but powerfully nostalgic smell."*

That smell ! *Perhaps nothing else so divides opinions about box. It has been "politely likened to foxes, but (is) really more like tom cat's urine" (Mabey). Queen Anne clearly shared this view, as she ordered much of the box topiary at Hampton Court to be removed because of its smell.*

And she was not alone. John Evelyn refers to the smell of box having "of late banished it from our Groves and gardens."

🌿 The 'fragrance of eternity'?

Yet others have different views.

The smell of box is said to be very evocative and able to conjure up visions of the past. Christopher Lloyd, in The Well-tempered Garden, *states that it "has a nostalgic charm for many people", adding, rather more practically, "perhaps, also for snails."*

The American writer, Oliver Wendell Holmes, in his 1861 novel, Elsie Venner, *took a romantic view. "They walked over the crackling leaves in the garden, between the lines of Box, breathing its fragrance of eternity ; for this is one of the odors which carry us out of time into the abysses of the unbeginning past…"*

🌿 Box Gardens of the past

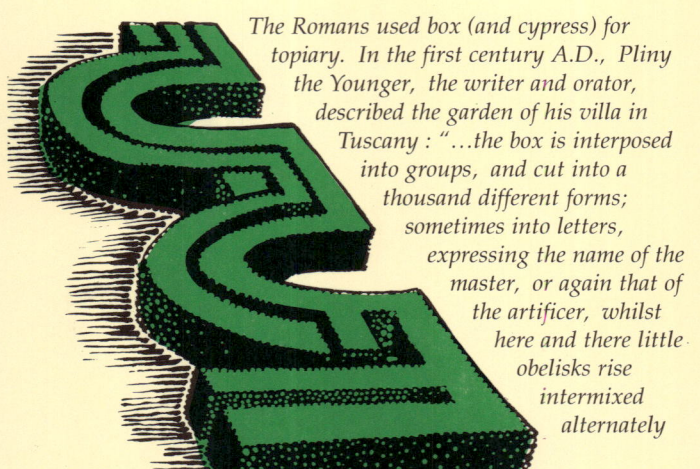

The Romans used box (and cypress) for topiary. In the first century A.D., Pliny the Younger, the writer and orator, described the garden of his villa in Tuscany : "…the box is interposed into groups, and cut into a thousand different forms; sometimes into letters, expressing the name of the master, or again that of the artificer, whilst here and there little obelisks rise intermixed alternately

with fruit-trees." He noted that box was traditionally watered with wine.

At Fishbourne Palace, near Chichester, there is a box garden following the original Roman planting, traces of which were found during excavations (see facing page).

These Roman skills were gradually lost, but the art of box topiary was rediscovered in the Renaissance. In England, the Elizabethan age saw great enthusiasm for knot gardens and low mazes - puzzles to delight the eye, not to confuse like later tall mazes. The development of a dwarf variety of box in Holland in the sixteenth century was ideal for knot gardens.

❧ Knot gardens

Knot gardens probably evolved from medieval kitchen gardens where medicinal and culinary herbs had to be kept separate from each other. They were very popular in the sixteenth and seventeenth centuries, and took several forms. The low box edging, in the form of knots or interlocking geometric shapes, surrounded flowering plants, gravel or other stones, or grass.

The early American colonists brought the idea of knot gardens with them, perhaps finding that they were a symbol of order in the surrounding untamed land. Thomas Jefferson's father owned a plantation at Tuckahoe in which there was an acre of knot garden. The box hedges, laid out in ovals and concentric circles, would have extended one-and-a-half miles if placed in a straight line.

Parterres

Similar to knot gardens but larger in scale, these were much developed by the French who greatly enlarged formal gardens during this period. By the early 1700s, three distinct types had appeared :

parterres de broderie, *consisting of box edging and coloured earth in an imitation of embroidery;*
parterres à l'anglaise, *where the box was used to edge turf cut into patterns;*
parterres of cut work, *where the box outlines were filled with flowers.*

Enthusiasm for parterres was widespread at this time. Records show that they existed in Germany, Sweden, Spain and Portugal as well as France and England. The idea even spread to China.

Some may still be seen. There are famous box parterres at Seaton Delaval Hall in Northumberland. At Pitmedden, in Aberdeenshire, the Scottish National Trust has a partly original, partly modern, box-edged parterre, in an attempt to guess what the seventeenth century originator would have done with modern plants.

However, many more parterres of this period have been lost. The heyday of formal gardens and topiary, during the reign of William and Mary, came to an end with the return to 'natural' landscaping. Blenheim originally had much parterre work, designed by Henry Wise, but this was removed by 'Capability' Brown (the existing parterres are Edwardian).

Other topiary

With its slow growth rate, box lends itself well to low topiary. It has been used for sundials, with the gnomon and numerals planted in box and the dial filled with light-coloured gravel to enable the shadow to show clearly. At the end of the nineteenth century, Lady Warwick wrote: "Never was such a perfect timekeeper as my sundial, and the figures are all cut out and trimmed in box."

Box can also be used for larger topiary, if the gardener has sufficient patience. Alexander Pope, in an attack on the artificiality of gardening in 1713, gives imaginary examples of topiary for sale. He describes a "catalogue of greens" from an "eminent town-gardener" who suggests that "the world stands much in need of a virtuoso gardener, who has a turn to sculpture, and is thereby capable of improving upon the ancients in the imagery of evergreens." Pope gives two alleged examples for box:"St George in box; his arm scarce long enough, but will be in a condition to stick the dragon by next April. A green dragon of the same, with a tail of ground-ivy for the present. N.B. These two are not to be sold separately."

🌿 Cultivation

Box is not difficult to establish in most cases, although some of the rarer species may have special requirements. The more common varieties, including the native British **Buxus sempervirens**, *are very hardy, tolerant of poor conditions and capable of growing in both dry areas such as Southern Italy and the cooler and wetter climes of more Northerly countries.*

More than eighty species of box are known to exist, in various parts of the world. The majority of these are obtainable in Britain but may not grow in exactly the same form if they originte from a different climatic zone. In particular, some of the rarer species are not winter-hardy in this country.*

There are dwarf boxes, boxes for hedging, boxes suitable for upright or columnar growth, pendulous boxes, boxes which form low mounds and those which are suitable for shaping. Some are particularly suited to container growing. Most have dark green foliage, but there are also variegated forms and some Asiatic species have paler leaves.

While particular species may have their own special requirements, there are many general points to make regarding the cultivation, clipping and propagation of box.

* *See note at the back.*

Growing conditions

Buxus sempervirens, *the Common Box, being native to chalkland, grows particularly well on alkaline soils but can easily be cultivated elsewhere. The same applies to other readily available species. The colour of the leaves may be affected by acid soil but the addition of a seaweed or dolomitic limestone fertiliser should counteract this. However, it is essential not to overfeed box as the plants can scorch badly. Granular fertiliser should be applied just outside the line of foliage in order to prevent damage to the sensitive surface-feeding roots.*

Similarly, box can tolerate both exposed and sheltered areas. If very exposed to sun and wind, it can become bronzed in colour and, for this reason, many gardeners prefer to grow it in light shade. Being a surface rooter, its rooting area should be kept cool and well aerated; another reason for growing it in some shade. It responds well to mulching but its own dead leaves should not be left underneath (or inside) the plant as this could encourage fungal diseases.

🌿 Containers

Box can be grown very successfully in containers provided it has enough space and nutrients. The pot should be several centimetres wider than the rootball, and large plants require even more room. After about three years, it is usually necessary either to change to a larger container or to root-prune the plant.

The compost should contain some loam (John Innes No.3 is successful). A top-dressing of blood, fish and bone (or a similar proprietary product), mixed with a little fresh compost, should be applied in spring. Liquid feeding with seaweed fertiliser is desirable in summer.

Since box foliage is dense, rain does not reach underneath if the plant is grown in a container. Watering is therefore very important, and the pot should be placed on a terracotta saucer so that the plant may take up water when it needs it. The saucer should be removed during the winter.

🌿 Pests & other problems

*The most common **pests** of box are psyllids (suckers, or jumping plant lice) which damage the appearance of the plant but do not affect its health. In spring, the emerging psyllid nymph feeds on the inside of the young leaves, creating a stunted 'Brussels sproat' effect with a fluffy white exudation. This can be removed by trimming.*

Other pests affecting the foliage are the box leafminer, which causes blistering on young leaves in the late summer, and the boxwood mite, which causes stippling of older leaves in summer.

Scale insects can cause die-back by taking sap from the plant. They appear as tiny, comma shaped, brown specks on the stems, and can be controlled by the use of insecticidal soap or horticultural oil. Other possible pests include webworms which may cause webs to form on the inner branches in summer.

Fungus infection *is particularly common in wet, warm summers, and can be recognised by sudden discolouration and loss of leaves. Early spraying with a systemic fungicide should be accompanied by the removal and burning of all dead leaves.*

Clipping

Since box is so widely used for topiary and as an edging plant, clipping is a matter of great importance. Ideally, it should be carried out twice a year, but this will depend on the length of the summer. The vital consideration is that all risk of frost should be past.

Frost damage *can be severe, and one frosty night can suffice. However fast the new, bright green leaves seem to be growing, and however untidy the plant may appear, it is generally best to wait until June, or even later in some areas, before making the first clipping of the year. If the box is clipped before the frosts have ended, the soft wood which has been exposed will scorch and the leaves will turn brown.*

There is also a danger of frost at the end of the summer, of course. The second clipping should therefore be carried out before the end of August, in order to give the box time to recover and for the exposed wood to harden sufficiently to cope with frost.

Heat damage *can also occur, and box should never be clipped on a hot day. Otherwise, the cut areas may scorch and turn brown.*

Clipping must be carried out with great care if the box is not to lose its crisp outlines. For this reason, electric hedgecutters are of limited value, although a skilful user may be successful with an established hedge or topiary.

Even ordinary garden shears can cause temporary damage. They should be as sharp as possible and handled with great care to avoid damaging the soft leaves. Cutting should take place on a line within the old growth.

Some experts recommend the American technique of plucking by hand rather than clipping, although this is not suitable if a very crisp outline is required. It is also quite hard work and difficult to carry out on a large number of plants. The method is very simple, with pieces about fifteen centimetres long being broken off the branches by hand. It encourages the plant to thicken by letting light and air in, and gives a fluffy, 'woolly' appearance.

Topiary

Box is ideal for hedging, knot gardens and parterres. Dwarf varieties, the most widely available being Buxus sempervirens *'suffruticosa', are particularly useful for edging. Larger-scale topiary, however, seems once again to divide opinion. Many topiarists consider yew to be the ideal plant for the purpose, being very malleable, but box also has its supporters. It is softer-textured than yew and more difficult to keep in shape, but many prefer its appearance. It is more generally recommended for small-scale work.*

Box can be very effective in simple shapes, such as cones, balls and obelisks, and can also be trained into spirals. It is, of course, possible to create animals and other objects. For example, one topiarist converted a neglected two-metre high Buxus sempervirens *into a monkey. Nathaniel Lloyd's 1925 book, "Craftsmanship in Yew and Box", was the first book for centuries to give detailed instructions for creating elaborate shapes but others have been published since.*

The temptation to clip box into shapes can be irrestible. In Flora Britannica, *Richard Mabey refers to topiary being practised on wild trees in France. He describes the discovery of carefully clipped bushes miles from any habitation, the topiarists being road-menders during their lunch breaks.*

❧ Propagation

Buxus sempervirens can be propagated by division of suckering roots, but an easier method is probably to take hardwood cuttings. Box is a very easy plant to raise in this manner.

Cuttings should be taken between July and September and be about fifteen centimetres long. The base leaves should be stripped off, leaving a stem with branchlets at the top. If a cut is then made below a bud or node, where the hormones are stored, no rooting powder is necessary.

The cuttings are best planted in ordinary soil, in open ground, and require shade to prevent scorching by the sun. An ideal spot would be against a North-facing wall.

Cuttings may also be planted in pots, but these require more attention. The earth must be kept moist and the leaves green and full of sap. A plastic cover or bag over the top can be useful for this. The use of gravelly sand will help the cuttings to root well.

"Ships of myrtle sail i

"All things considered, there is nothing neater, better, or more appropriate for all descriptions of garden edgings than box." (James Anderson, The New Practical Gardener and Modern Horticulturalist, 1871).

Unfortunately, there is a price to be paid for growing box for hedging and edging. It is a great attractor of snails, which is a major deterrent to its use in formal potagers. As a hedge, it tends to collect weeds: "Rare is the box hedge that has not accumulated within it a nucleus of ground elder, bindweed or couch…" (Christopher Lloyd, The Well-tempered Garden) and these of course spread readily to neighbouring flowerbeds.

But for the devotee of box, these things do not matter. The effort involved is well compensated by the beauty of the result. The seventeenth century French poet, René Rapin, must have been just such an enthusiast, as he wrote of the origin of boxwood in gardens :

> *The goddess Flora's hair was always untidy, until a nymph arranged it for her and tied the tresses with a wreath of boxwood. This so transformed the goddess's beauty that the plant has ever since been used to trim beds "where flowers disordered once in random grew".*

eas of box" *(Homer, The Odyssey)*

Botanical Notes

Common name:
   Box or Common Box;
   sometimes Boxwood

Botanical name:
   Buxus sempervirens

Family: Buxaceae

Growth: Very slow-growing. Seedlings have two deciduous leaves before the true leaves develop.

Size: Height up to ten metres, girth less than one metre. Smaller varieties more usual in gardens.

Leaves: Evergreen. Small (about 2 cm long), ovate, leathery, set in opposite pairs. Dark green and glossy on the upper side, paler below. Buds very small.

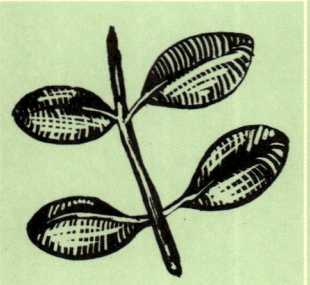

Special characteristic: Box has the densest wood of any native British tree and does not float in water even when fully seasoned.

Sub-varieties: There are more than twenty-five cultivars or 'types' of Buxus sempervirens readily available in Britain. The traditional dwarf box is Buxus sempervirens 'suffruticosa', which means 'small and shrubby'.

Flowers: Inconspicuous. Small, greenish, set in clusters of both male and female in the leaf axils. Flowers from January to May.

Fruit: Ripens from August to September or October. Six hard black seeds contained in a three-celled, white pod with three double-pointed horns.

Bark: Grey, fine-textured, often in a small mesh pattern.

The other boxwoods usually available in this country include varieties of Buxus microphylla, or Japanese box. More recently, varieties of Buxus sinica, the common box of China, have become obtainable.

In the same series

Cedar of Lebanon
Holly
Oak

To be published soon

Ash • *Beech* • *Birch* • *Catalpa* • *Elm* • *Hawthorn*
Hornbeam • *Monkey Puzzle*
Mulberry • *Scots Pine* • *Willow* • *Yew*

If you enjoyed this book and would like
to buy any of the above titles
or require further information
please contact

SAGE PRESS

PO Box Nº 1, Rye, East Sussex TN36 4ZX.
e-mail: summertime @ lineone.net
Freephone number 0800 092 33 31

* For advice on the cultivation of box, contact the
National Box Collection,
Langley Boxwood Nursery,
Rake, Liss, Hampshire, GU33 7JL.
Tel: 44 (0) 1730 894467
Fax: 44 (0) 1730 894703